45 MINUTES

You are probably wondering about what I'm going to say right now. I dare not keep you in suspense. Tuck away in this book titled *When Sons Return Home* is my experience that only lasted forty-five minutes. I remember back in 1973 when I joined the army after finishing high school, I came home on leave in 1974 to visit my family and friends. Along with my brother James Lee and a host of high school buddies, we decided to attend the football game at the school we graduated from. I was happy to see them. Of course, we all were around nineteen years of age and some twenty, and we were also drinking and smoking marijuana. As we arrived at the school, we gathered around a building on the football field, where we again were smoking and drinking. I took some rolling papers out and began rolling a joint. At that time, the police officers rushed in, and everyone began to run. I dropped the joint, and before I could run, I was busted, handcuffed, placed in a police car, and hauled off to jail. I had never been to jail in my life. As we arrived in jail, they took me inside, fingerprinted me, and put me in a cell with other offenders. Trembling and scared in a white jeans outfit, I looked around the cell. One man had just shot his wife, another walked around with no clothes on, and the other one was a homosexual. I was in jail.

They let me make one phone call to my mother, and she said, "I'm coming to get you because you don't belong there."

Forty-five minutes later, they called my name, and I yelled, "Here I am!"

They opened the cell and brought me out to my mother. I was so glad to see my mother, and I told her that I was sorry for what I had done. I promised her that I would never go to jail again. From that point on, I made up my mind to do all I can to stay out of jail. It only took forty-five minutes to make up my mind. I didn't know enough about God, so I said, "Lord, have mercy. I'm in jail." Forty-five minutes later, when I came to my senses, I made up my mind.

PAGE PUBLISHING
Conneaut Lake, PA

First originally published by Page Publishing 2024

ISBN 979-8-89157-334-5 (pbk)
ISBN 979-8-89157-352-9 (digital)

Printed in the United States of America

WHEN SONS RETURN HOME

John B. Murray Sr.

*Your children will soon return to you, and the people
who defeated You and destroyed you will leave.*

—Isaiah 49:17–18

CONTENTS

ACKNOWLEDGMENTS

This book would not be what it is intended to be without the tremendous amount of assistance from various pastors, family and friends, and various authors who were willing to share with me wisdom to write.

As always, I'm profoundly thankful for and grateful to the love and support of my wife, Brenda Murray. Without her long-suffering and faithful encouragement, I could not endure the rigors of writing in addition to my duties of being a pastor.

INTRODUCTION

As I pondered the title of this book, I thought of my own sons and what experiences we encountered as a family. Our home was never the image of heaven, nor was it the image of hell. We were typically a family that had love, respect, compassion, support, correction, discipline, and our fair share of mistakes and failures. We knew what it was to experience broken fellowship through the grace and mercy of God. It's God who handpicks who would be our biological family on this earth. These special people share a bond like no other, and it's a relationship that can truly affect the rest of our lives.

All families start out with a good relationship, and overtime, if it goes unnoticed, selfishness, disobedience, rebellion, and feud can cause relationships to suffer and lose the strength that it once had. Family structure can become severed when any of the family members behaves in such a counter-harmonious fashion. Perhaps you came from a broken family or in one right now. Thank God that the Word of God reveals vital tools that can help you build or rebuild the happy family God wants you to have. A family's health and happiness can be broken by someone in the family who wants to live their lives as they see fit despite who has the authority over them. No one comes from a perfect background. The prodigal's story can shine some light on family breakups and what it takes to make up or mend up. What kind of sons return home?

CHAPTER 1

The Prodigal Type of Son

As I began to write this book, *When Sons Return Home*, it prompted me to ask a serious question: What was the home like when the prodigal left home, and what was the home like when the prodigal returned home?

Every Christian who has a relationship with God and who knows God understands that God gives everyone the gift of "free will." The reason why the prodigal son could not remain at home to live a sinful life was very apparent, but not specifically stated. I was able to visually see in this story, in this home, that as a Christian Father, he set definitive boundaries in what a person could do and not do within his home, according to the Word of God.

Again, God gives us all, every one of us, free will, and as we mature to a certain age, we have to be responsible for our own individual actions. When the prodigal son's sinful ways were exhausted for various reasons, blessed was he that he had a godly family to come home to. Vice versa, blessed was his family that the prodigal son had to learn valuable lessons that on his own cognitive he wanted to come home and live a righteous life.

Every parent understands that their sons and daughters can be wayward or become wayward. The Word of God reminds us that God has situations in line for anyone who is wayward, to learn certain life lessons, so they will surrender to God's perfect love.

Yet we do understand that not everyone responds to God's love, and that person can hinder God's work in their lives. The story of the prodigal son is a parable from God that can be applied to so many areas in our lives. We have yet to find out if the prodigal son had other resources, friends, and/or family members facilitating his sinful ways. The prodigal son might not have ever come home. As you examine your own household, you can never forget that setting boundaries according to God's Word to what a person can do and cannot do is a vital part of loving those we love.

What would you say if God's Word says that you can do anything that you please? God breathed His Word into the writers of the Bible for so many reasons, including setting boundaries. Why? To save us from ourselves and to save us from the devil's grip. Did you know that you can aid or help Satan by doing your own loved ones in when you facilitate, purposely overlook, aid, assist, abet, or help a person's sinful lifestyle to continue by willfully choosing to never set boundaries especially when you are in a position to do so?

Can we talk for a minute?

I have personally met a number of people (i.e., pastors, deacons, ushers, choir members, family, and friends) who testified that they had recognized after the fact that for years and various reasons, they thought they were helping a family member, but they really were destroying that family member by assisting their sinful lifestyle. The Word of God will teach you about the many ways of having dignity.

The Bible also teaches us that some of the ways are to have respect for God, respect for God's Word, and respect for ourselves by the way we conduct ourselves, by the way we treat others, and for the most part, showing love by setting boundaries especially when we are put in a position to do so. Yes, we have to be careful to not let our love for someone cause us to accept or put up with their sins by offering our houses and providing our finances or other assistance, hindering those perfect life lessons that God creates to have a relationship with him.

God's entire Bible, in particular the book of Proverbs, provides the godly wisdom to address set plans for social issues that we might have, as well as setting boundaries as to what a person can or cannot do in your household.

Every child of God in a leadership role should have zero tolerance in their household for willful sinning without repentance.

Can we talk?

What if you didn't know right from wrong and you sinned openly and you didn't have anyone who loved you enough to correct you or lead you by example? Can you imagine being head of a household that's void of biblical standards of what someone could or could not do? Have you ever had to tell someone in your household the following: "We do not allow this in our house."

In your home, where you are in a position of authority, God teaches us that we should love each other enough to set boundaries so that if you have wayward family members, they have a Christian home they can hold on to or they can come home if need be.

I believe that God omitted other characters in the story of the prodigal son and his sinful ways as an example for us of what not to do. So many people have worn their patience thin while a wayward son or daughter chooses to live a lifestyle of sin. Yes, it can be difficult and, in many cases, a painful experience.

Yet the only thing we can do besides setting an example of someone living a Christian lifestyle is to put our trust in God and pray in great conviction that God would create a perfect life lesson for our loved one to repent and turn their life over to God.

So when the prodigal left home and returned, the father's Christian standards never changed. It was a godly home when he left and was a godly home when he returned.

My question is this: What did the prodigal son hope to gain by leaving home in Luke 15:11–27?

As we read the story of the prodigal son, we are not told about his accomplishments or goals or the good things he did at home. So you and I have to use our own humanology and understanding to see what his motivation was.

For a minute, let's hear it from a mother's point of view. There was nothing wrong at home, but he wanted more than what he had at home. So he ventured out thinking that he could find more out there than he had at home. In his eyes, he was somewhat limited at home, and by leaving home, nothing was kept back from him. He could jump in with all four feet and not have to answer to anybody.

Let's hear it from a father's point of view. He thought he was missing something. He lived near Babylon, and in Babylon, they partied all night. He could lay in his bed at night and see and hear the lights and music. Babylon was the nightspot at that time. Whatever you want to do, you can do that in Babylon. Everyone he knew was at the party in Babylon, drinking, smoking, dancing, getting high, hanging out on corners, dressed in their best clothing, and getting into everything imaginable. That was fun that he didn't want to miss. His father wasn't having it. I could hear his father saying, "Boy, it's not all that it appears to be." The trap is to get you in there, but you don't know how you're going to come out.

So many fathers have told their sons this: "I've been there and done that." Well, did that give them the motivation to go out there and see for themselves how it really is so they could make a decision which way to go in life?

Let's go back into the home. We are still looking for some reasons that the prodigal son might have hoped to gain by leaving the home of his father.

His father was successful and rich. He did what was right in the eyes of God, and God blessed him, not only spiritually but materially. The father was able to put up an inheritance for both of his sons. The older son always carried himself in an obedient manner and never brought disappointment to his father. Maybe the prodigal son felt overshadowed by his father and older brother. Like so many of us, he wanted to make his own way in the world so he could feel important in his own right. This way, he could hope to gain more self-worth. If you talk with the prodigal son, he would tell that he felt like there was not going to be a place for him in his father's house because as a second son, there was no way that he was going to be the head of the family and that he would remain in a subordinate position all his life. This was a way he could hope to gain some independence by leaving to live on his own.

Let's see if we can make sense of this and then try to answer this question: When the prodigal son left home, why didn't someone go to find him?

In the book of Luke, chapter 15, Jesus presents three parables of something that is *lost*, being *found*. As you know, the first is a lost sheep, the second is a lost coin, and the third is a lost son. When the first two are found, there is a calling for others to rejoice with the person who found what had been lost.

Luke 5:6 ESV says, "And when he comes home, he calls together his friends and his neighbors, saying to them, 'rejoice with me, for I have found my sheep that was lost.'"

Luke 15:9 ESV says, "And when she has found it, she calls together her friends and neighbors, saying, 'rejoice with me, for I have found the coin that I had lost.'"

Look with me in this third parable. Why is it that we didn't see anyone finding the son, who the father said was lost, but there was a celebration when he was found? There it is, in the first two parables. Jesus reveals that somebody took action to find what was lost. Okay, when the father lost his son, did he or anyone else went to search for him? Let's walk in the father's shoes. I see frustration, and I see a father fed up with the attitude of the son. I see an angry son telling his father, "I don't want to live under your rules anymore."

Can't you hear the son saying, "Dad I wish you were dead. You are in the way of how I want to live my life. I want to be free of what's best for my life. My life doesn't involve this family. I want what I want for my life, and I have other plans that don't involve you."

How would you feel if your son said that to you after all you did for him? He also shows no gratitude in his heart and no genuine love for his father. Would you agree that any son who dishonors his father to the degree that this son has done deserves to be dispossessed of everything he had and then dismissed from the family? In Jesus's eyes, the father, as the family patriarch, is to be highly honored. The father was left with no other choice but to let him go.

In a culture where honor was so important, every father was expected to remain in charge and finally responsible for the household and all its assets until he died.

The first two parables noted that when they realized something was missing, they searched until they found it.

Stay with me. The prodigal son in Luke 15:11–31 appears to be a different picture. The son as you know voluntarily and purposely left to go to a far country and knew exactly where he was all the time he was gone.

This made it somewhat easy to go back to his father's house after he realized he made a mistake. When the son did not want to be found, why would anyone try to find him? When the sheep is separated from the flock, it has no thoughts on trying to get back. The sheep will wander around endlessly until someone looks for it and brings it back to the shepherd.

Well, man is not like a sheep. Man has reasoning power higher than that of a sheep and other animals. Man must be convinced in his own mind to willingly, on his own, go back to his father.

The father did not seek for his son like the shepherd and his sheep and the woman and her piece of money. The father did not want to deal with an irrational (unreasonable, absurd, foolish) son but with a rational (sound, wise, sober, sensible, sane, intelligent) son who must be allowed to choose, for himself, the right path to travel, which leads to the truth. The father was not working for his son's recovery but allowed him to bear all the consequences of his transgressions. Yet the father has been waiting patiently and all the while keeping his heart together and his home open to his son.

The prodigal son went off on his own and on his own came back to his father. The father going after his son would not have helped the situation because the son needed the time to realize the error of his ways. The son asked for his independence and was granted what he asked for.

What kind of son will return home after he made a mess of his life? He is the kind of son who realized he lost something valuable in his life.

The prodigal son's life eventually became a nightmare. He obviously made some dumb choices that opened the door for divine providence to make his troubles more dramatic than he could ever imagined. He finally saw life at its worst.

He left a good Christian home and a wonderful future provided by a godly, caring, loving, thoughtful, and generous father, and the scene turned into disaster.

CHAPTER 2

The Abuser Type of Son (Luke 15:13)

Let's examine the meaning of the word *prodigal*. The word *prodigal* means "spending money or resources freely and recklessly, wastefully extravagant." The most common answers are "rebellious" or "a runaway." Somewhere in the context of this famous parable, the *prodigal son* also means "someone who is spiritually lost and someone who has returned after an absence."

A prodigal is a person who leaves home and behaves recklessly but later makes a repentant return. He is someone who wastes and squanders what is given to him, someone who doesn't count the cost before taking action. The main thought behind the word *prodigal* is that of wastefulness, immoderation, excess, and dissipation. The *Cambridge Dictionary* meaning reads: "a man or boy has left his family in order to do something that the family disapprove of and has now returned home feeling sorry for what he has done."

Prodigality means the quality of spending or using large amounts of money, time, energy, etc., especially in a way that is not wise. It indicates the quality of a person who drives forth his money and who wastes it by spending with reckless abandon.

In this parable, the younger son demands "the share of property that falls to me" (v. 12). That means, he is asking for one-third of the father's possessions that he would ordinarily get when the father dies. He's asking for it now before his father is dead. Think about that.

How would you feel if your disobedient child confronted you with this suggestion? What would be your response? This father does the unthinkable; he granted it. Does it remind you of the amazing generosity that God shows toward us? Even when we are acting as selfishly as the prodigal son, God grants it to us.

God gives us what is his and allows us to misuse it out of respect for the freedom that he has given us. You have to understand that God knows that the misuse of our freedom will have no better results than it did with the prodigal son's misuse of his freedom and God trusts that we will learn our lesson and come back to him.

This parable is based on real-life situations where so many often veer off the expected path of events in surprising ways and those surprises teach us lessons. After he gets his share of his father's estate, he takes everything he has and goes "into a far country, and there he squanders his property in loose living." He falls into the shoes of an abuser. He abuses everything that was holy and voluntarily goes into a Gentile, pagan country, where he could live loosely without being judged by the people around him. He wanted to get out of God's land so that he could live in sin and fund his sinful lifestyle by what he took from his father.

Let's look into the mind of an abuser. The abuser will often retreat into an attitude of arrogance and denial. Some abusers refuse to acknowledge their pathological and unhealthy behaviors toward others, especially to those of the same household. The best way to deny they are the problem is to get rid of you or get from around you. Abuse can come in multiple forms, and in this case, it was verbal abuse. We don't know how long the father had to deal with his son's verbal abuse.

He doesn't simply vanish from the community, but he stays around a couple of days to auction off the father's possessions that have just been handed down to him. As he sells at discount his inheritance to make cash, he is publicly putting his father to shame. When his disgraceful deed is done, the prodigal heads off to the far country.

Sin can lead you into the cheapening of God's gift. Man constantly will abuse God's blessings. We all have gone into the far country of exile. After abusing God's blessings, we squander our lives away in short-term thrills, which bring lifelong misery.

We all benefit from his gifts in every way possible without ever thinking about how God wants us to take care of them. The prodigal son was defiant and portrays mental abuse. Let's list some ways that the prodigal son displayed mental abuse:

1. Disobedience to rules and crossing boundaries
2. Disrespect for authority
3. Unteachable and unable to accept responsibility
4. Self-derived behavior (drugs, drinking, violence)

All these on the list sound like most of our abusers today. When the abusers feel like they do not have full control, they will try to break you down from the inside out, starting with your mind. Mental abuse makes you have many different feelings. I've discovered that abusers are out for themselves and they don't have anyone else's interest in mind. The behavior of abusers comes from a belief of superiority or a sense of entitlement.

Abusers are very good at manipulating their victims into knowing how to please them and appease their needs. Abusers begin to dehumanize their victim. This is the reason why the longer you are in a relationship (parent, spouse, child, etc.) with an abuser, the worse the abuse gets. This was another form of dishonor displayed by the prodigal son. This is so amazing as we remind ourselves that Jesus is giving us an illustration of his own love for sinners. Jesus, the Son of God, is God incarnate, the Lord himself in human form. It's here that we understand that the reaction of the prodigal's father represents the love of God for rebellious humanity. God extends to every man, woman, boy, and girl a generous measure of mercy, loving kindness, goodwill, and long-suffering.

But dishonor was beneath Christ, who walked out of heaven and away from his rightful position as God. The Bible tells us: "He made Himself of no reputation, taking the form of a bondservant, and coming in the likeness of man, and being found in appearance as a man, He humbled Himself and became obedient unto death, even the death of the cross" (Philippians 2:7–8).

Every abuser is given the chance to turn to God or return to God when they finally realize that they have shamed God, shamed their parents, and shamed themselves. Let's consider James 4:1–5. What causes quarrels and fights among you? Is it not this that your passion are at war within you? You desire and do not have, so you murder. You covet and cannot obtain, so you fight and quarrel. You do not have because you do not ask. You ask and do not receive because you ask wrongly to spend it on your passion, you, adulterous people! Do you not know that friendship with the world is enmity with God? Therefore, whoever wishes to be friends of the world makes himself an enemy of God, or do you suppose it is to no purpose that the scripture says, "He yearns jealously over the spirit that he has made to dwell in us?"

CHAPTER 3

The Lost Son

In this lesson, we will look at the lost son and examine how the son was lost and then sought the father's mercy. Most of us will go through a time when we feel lost, a time when we might even cause our lostness, our distance, from God. It's important that we learn that when we reject God's command, the teaching of our Lord and Savior Jesus Christ, and the tenants of our faith, we all will become lost and distant from the love and joy of our God's house. Now we face the consequences of sin and rejecting God's ways. You end up physically empty and spiritually lost.

The prodigal son is a lost son, and also he is a picture of any of us who are sinners, willful, neglectful, and indifferent to the teaching of Jesus and the love of God.

Who are you in this story? Are you a prodigal, a pharisee, or a servant? Are you the rebellious son, lost and far from God, a sinner, sinful, and sinning? Are you the self-righteous son, like the pharisee, who is no longer capable of rejoicing when a sinner returns to God? Are you the son or daughter who has hit rock-bottom and came to his/her senses and decided to run to God's open arms of compassion and mercy—you who was lost and now broken and seeking forgiveness and mercy? Finally, are you one of the servants in the father's house, rejoicing with the father when a lost son finds his way back home?

Let's be real today, have you ever been lost, angry, and struggling to find your way, hardened on the outside yet deeply bruised and hurting on the inside? Not only were you suffering from the pain of your choices, but you created pain and heartache in your family. You helped cut the cord that held relationships together.

Are you someone or a parent who never gave up on your children despite how rough it has been? I challenge you as a father to take up your arms and fight the spiritual battle that rages over your son or daughter with all your God-given strength. Every parent makes it their business to try to figure out what is going on in their sons' and daughters' lives and think about how to solve the problem. This is when you will experience a high degree of trouble, attacks, and mysterious afflictions. Then one day, when you look around and they are no longer there, it symbolizes that the hands of the enemy have arrested your child.

When the son or daughter is lost, there is a spiritual meaning.

1. It means you have lost your blessings.
2. It symbolizes a witchcraft plan to exchange the original glory of your son or daughter.
3. It indicates that you have lost someone important.
4. It says that you lack peace, joy, and happiness.
5. It means that your son will pass through a series of difficulties and downfalls from bad decisions.
6. It's a clear indication that your son will be great in life.
7. It means a son's lostness can make that son not have a good relationship with the father.
8. It can also mean, depending on the seriousness of the matter, that your son will likely disown you in the future.

I think every father needs to pray continuously for themselves and their family in the blood of Jesus. I believe that God will surely answer if you are consistent with your prayers. To be spiritually lost is to deny that man was created in the image of God. We, in all our selves and in all our different parts of life, are the image of God in the world and cannot deny this. Being spiritually lost is to reject who and what one is and, therefore, to become double-minded or without the capacity to think properly.

Jesus tells these parables in the Bible, and it relates to this awful condition of being lost. All people, and I mean all of us, live in sin; we are sinners. Without God's salvation plan for us, we would be condemned, and our eternal future would be sealed in the lake of fire with Satan and his angels.

The sin that man does is against God, and it makes us enemies of God, but our salvation to be made right and cleansed is not in the capability of man but must come to us by God, and it has to be in his terms.

Every child of God realizes that God is "Top Authority" and "Supreme Authority." He has freedom from all "outside" allegiance and has the right to self-govern. So God's sovereignty means he is free to do what he desires without any fear of human assistance or foreign interference. Sovereignty in salvation is God's work, salvation is God's plan, and it is his pleasure and desire to give man salvation through his grace and mercy and love through the work of Jesus Christ on the cross.

God is sovereign in all things. In his determination to save, he means that every man would remain ignorant, spiritually lost, bound in sin, and set to face God's eternal judgment.

For every lost soul that comes to Jesus for salvation and every new soul that is saved and enters into the kingdom of heaven, all the angels in heaven rejoice over one that comes.

John 3:16 sums it up: "For God so loved the world that he gave His only begotten Son, that whosoever believes in Him should not perish but have everlasting life."

The lost can come back to God by faith because, without faith, it is impossible to please God.

CHAPTER 4

The Reality Type of Son

Luke 15:17 says, "But when He came to himself." What happens when you focus on one thing so intensely that you miss other important things? Have you ever had a friend say, "Man, I saw you pass by. I waved, and I called your name, but you never turned around." Whatever you were concentrating on blocked your view of someone waving at you. You were locked into a train of thought and didn't notice anything else.

I am a witness to having experienced this in my life, where me, myself, and I was locked into a state of mind. Yes, in pursuit of what I wanted, no one close to me could get my attention, not even God. It happens in all our lives when we are hell-bent on our own plans, assuming that it will lead to happiness. God's ways and God's plan do not always point in the direction we want to go. It's at that point that we begin to map out our own course while convincing ourselves that God is involved in it. It's not God's will that we want, but it's our own will that we want to be done.

When I think about the prodigal son in Luke 15, it amazed me how much I am like him. Maybe you are like him. If you have been there, then you would agree with me at that time in our lives we wanted to plot our own course, disregard God's plan, and decide to call our own shots. We had our eyes on our own plans and couldn't see anything else. Lo and behold, things started to crumble, like it did for the prodigal son. It needed to happen, and that's when I came to my senses.

When I came to myself, when the prodigal came to himself, we begin to realize that when all the dust settles, our own plans fail. We are in the shoes of the prodigal now, where we recognize that we have sinned and strayed away from God. When things began to unravel, we were open to seeing things differently. All the things we thought were worth adventuring left us empty and desperate. And what about the hurt and pain we took our loved ones through?

The prodigal son has a chance to make things right. He has a chance to turn from his sin and turn back to his father and to God. Look at what the prodigal son did at the lowest part of his life. He knew where real love and real living was, and he realized that he did fail at that moment, at that unthinkable time in his life. *He came to himself.* As my father would say, "He came to his senses."

We ought to acknowledge that God knows best and that no one else but us are responsible for everything that went wrong in our lives. Maybe it was that career that didn't bring honor to God or those distractions that snatched us away from righteousness, holiness, and obedience or that no good relationship that overpowered important priorities in our lives.

Whatever it was that took the prodigal out and away from that which was good and decent, he chose it. It's hard to say I lost it all and to make things right, but we need to own that. The prodigal had to backtrack, own his failures, and make his way back to where he should have been all the time. He only needed to come back to his senses. He realized that where he ended up was not the place he wanted to be. Away from his father was worse than being where his father was, back home.

In saving our souls, what two things should we know? First is to know God, and second is to know ourselves. The two have to relate to one another. If you know only about God, you will be filled with pride, and your soul will be paralyzed. If you know only about your sins and your unworthiness and know little about God, you will be filled with despondency and fear and/or escapism, and again, your soul will be paralyzed, unable to do good.

Despondency (loss of hope) is common among mankind to a greater or lesser degree. If it happens to you to a greater degree, you won't be saved because you won't be able to do the things you need to do to learn. But if you learn about yourself and God at the same time, God will reveal himself.

The son was the problem, and he had to see himself to come to himself. He realized just how far his sinful passions took him—far away. He piled sin upon sin in his soul, and now, he must painfully take off, one stone at a time. So the more we pile on ourselves, the more difficult it becomes and further away we are and the further we must travel back.

Yes, things change when you hit rock-bottom, and there is no place to look but up. When you are at a low point in your life, don't lose hope, and don't despair. Jesus reveals this parable to encourage us to remember that true love and true forgiveness is at home. Realization of how things really are out in an unforgiving world will quickly change your mind. The prodigal son found himself chasing the pleasures of the world in order to find satisfaction, until he realized that peace is not found in possessions, wild living, or money. It is found in meaningful relationships with our Creator and with our loved ones. We all have issues that require attention. We all have sins that need to be brought to the Lord. When he came to himself, it was a reminder that it's not too late to change and start over with God's help. The fact of the matter is that neither you nor I nor the prodigal son deserves grace and mercy. We have been given exactly that through the death and resurrection of Jesus Christ. When life gets bad enough, it causes us to immerse ourselves in the highness of God's ultimate sacrifice that we begin to experience the compassion and wisdom of the Father in this parable.

God's love for us is unconditional. God loves us whether we are the greatest saints in the world or the biggest sinners to walk the earth. It's we as humans who put the labels and categories on people. God's unyielding and unconditional love is a challenge for us to go the extra mile when it comes to looking into the minds and hearts of our family and friends.

So many times, it is our limited and human ways of looking at things that cut us off from seeing things through the magnetic eyes of God. That's why, it is so easy to divide people into good and bad, winners and losers, and successful and unsuccessful. It's our way but not God's way. Christianity involves a radical belief system, and if we are serious about it, we have to be struck in awe at how it brings us to the reality of how life really is.

There is no limit to love, and there is no time when a Christian can say enough is enough. It's true Christianity offers mankind the never-ending possibility of accepting the Lord and Savior as Christ. Thank God that there are no conditions and no small-worded documentations. It's God that loves us regardless of the state we find ourselves in. The Bible says that God's ways are not our ways; therefore, it is impossible for us to understand yet comprehend how God can love sinners, losers, and wasters.

The Word of God tells us it's on the side of the poor and the slaves and sinners. Thank God that he is in the midst of the lowliest. The Bible was never written for us to look down on the faults of others or whoever is the cream in our world.

The prodigal son came to reality in a faraway place, with people he didn't know anything about, and he thought he could stay anonymous, with money to burn, no consequences or responsibilities, no one looking over his shoulders, not even his father.

Reality dawned on him after he spent all his time looking for paradise, and when he arrived, it looked like he found it, and he gave no thought to the future. He thought he had all things in his hand, yet it was only for a little while.

Reality set in, and reality struck. All of a sudden, he had no money, no food, no friends, and no family, not even his father. The Word of God reminds us that God is merciful. God allowed the vault of his heaven to collapse. He allowed the bright sunshine to turn into night. God allowed his restless heart to convict him of his own vanity.

What he never expected to find was now staring him in the face unasked for and unlooked for: the grace of repentance. What he was about to eat, he would have never eaten at his father's house. What was unthinkable at this moment, nostalgia for his father's house seized him.

My thought is: "Everybody has to choose to leave, and everybody has to leave and come back so they can love it again for all the new reasons."

Thank you, Lord. Here is the God I want to believe in, a Father who, from the beginning of creation, has stretched out his arms in merciful blessing, never forcing himself on anybody but constantly waiting and never letting his arms droop in despair but always hoping that his children will return so that he can speak words of love to them and his arms on their shoulders. God's only desire is to bless.

The prodigal son is a reality for so many of us. In the path of life, we quickly realize that there are no guarantees as a Christian parent. No matter how hard we strive to teach our children about God and his Word and no matter how much we pray for our children to seek Jesus Christ and the way to salvation, some of our prodigals choose to reject it all.

Even in those households where God is worshipped and praised, trusted, and glorified, they often rebel and leave their roots. The road to recovery is when they realized that wrong choices lead to wrong places and doing wrong things. This son finally realized that God alone is Lord.

We are hypocrites when we pretend to be something we are not. The reality is, we've all had our moments of dissolute living to some degree. We all have received some compensation for those things we have done and those things we have left undone.

I believe that in various parts of our lives, we are the father, the prodigal, and the older son, and isn't it amazing that the prodigal son ends up spiritually made over again and healthier when all the dust settles? If we all desire human perfection, it will manifest itself by the way we handle our own imperfection. This is something we learn about the prodigal son: recognizing how we handle the imperfection of our lives. You see it right there in the story; the prodigal finally comes to grips with his own imperfections.

Can I be real for a moment? As hypocritical as some of us are, none of us wants to be known or found in our worst moments. You know as well as I know that we look for the best way to cover our guilty selves, and that is to expose the guilt of other people. This means that we are still in the closet, hiding the real us, the abuser us, the low-self-esteem us, the follow-the-crowd us, the deceptive us, the insecure us, the low-down us, the hell-raiser us, the doubtful us, the hot-tempered us, the mean-spirited us, the evil-thinking us, the disobedient us, and the nonbelieving us. It's the actual us. None of us are perfect and beyond reproach. We have so artfully constructed our false selves that we end up crippling ourselves. I believe that we all have to experience a major crisis before we can engage in the self-examination that is required to get back to reality.

I remember as a young boy, we went to the county fair, and I loved to ride the merry-go-round, and if you could touch the brass rings, I mean reach out far enough and grab the brass ring, you could win a prize. I later found out that the words *grabbing the brass ring* meant "striving for the highest prize or living life to the fullest."

I've discovered that the brass ring is compared to our life with God, where we live the fullness of an authentic life with God, a holy life where we can stop pretending and be who we really are in Christ. Every day that God wakes us up, we ride the merry-go-round of life as we reach out to grab hold of God's unchanging hand (the brass ring) and let go of the superficial things of ourselves and face reality that God is God and he alone has all power in his hand. Here's where I am convinced that true repentance always begins with an accurate assessment of your own condition. Let's be clear: when the prodigal son faced the reality of his own condition, it caused a monumental change in his attitude toward his father.

How many of us have put up a fuss when it's time to take a look at the situation we are in? I mean facing the ugly reality and accepting responsibility for what we have done, owning up to the seriousness of our guilt, admitting that we are helpless, and now turning to somebody who can help us through it all.

Do you have a plan B in place after you realize how messed up you are and all the mess you caused in the family? Plan A—you wanted your own way, you did what pleases you, and you went where all the excitement was so you could do like everybody else, party hardy. Now that you are at the end of that road, things didn't go like you thought. The world pulled a wool over your eyes, blinding you to how life really is down in the dumps. What's plan B?

The prodigal had a plan B. He came to himself, and he faced reality. The father also faced reality that the only way to make his son understand what was good for him was to let him learn through his own experiences.

CHAPTER 5

The Made-Up-Mind Type of Son

The prodigal son is still teaching us lessons about his life and how quickly you and I can fall into his shoes. He reminds us, "Lost people matter to god." God is not the kind of God to leave you in the state that you are in. Even in our rebellious state of mind, God finds ways to bring us to our senses. Every one of us had to get to this point where we needed to make up our minds about whether to stay at the lowest part of our lives or get up and go back to what has always been best for us.

What an amazing thought: Lost People Matter To God. The Bible in 2 Peter 3:9 says, "The Lord is not slack concerning His promise, as some count slackness, but is longsuffering toward us, not willing that any should perish but that all should come to repentance."

What an amazing thought: Lost People Matter To God. John 3:16 says: "For God so loved the world that he gave His only begotten Son, that whoever believes in him should not perish but have everlasting life."

Here is another amazing thought: *God should matter to lost people.* Every man, woman, boy, and girl should have it written in their minds and on their hearts: *I need God!* A mind that is away from God is a mind against God.

Romans 8:7–8 says, "The carnal mind is enmity against God; for it Is not subject to the law of God, nor indeed can be. So then, those who are in the flesh cannot please God." The apostle Paul explains in Romans chapter one that the wrath of God is revealed from heaven against all unrighteousness of man. He also lists the reason: although they knew God, they refused to honor God as God or give thanks to God. Our unrighteousness does not manifest itself in our far country, but our unrighteousness is seen when we refuse to honor God for what he has done in our lives.

The prodigal made up his mind when life caught up with him. Luke 15:14–17 says:

> And when he had spent everything, a severe famine arose in that country, and he began to be in need. So he went and hired out one of the citizens of that country, who sent him into his field to feed pigs. And he was longing to be fed with the pods that the pigs ate, and no one gave him anything.
>
> But when he came to himself, he said, "How many of my father's hired servants have more than enough bread, but I perish here with hunger."

He was so desperate that he almost fought the pigs over the slop he was supposed to feed them with. So he made up his mind. "I can't live like this anymore. I will arise and go to my father's house. I need God."

Words of wisdom: Don't you ever try to put anyone or anything ahead of God. Never put your children ahead of God because you're going to need God to help you when those children go crazy. Don't you ever try to put your job ahead of God because you are going to need God when they lay you off that job. Don't you ever try to put your spouse ahead of God because you are going to need God when they cheat on you with another man or woman. Don't you ever try to put your friends ahead of God because you are going to need God when they stab you in the back. Don't you ever try to put material things ahead of God because you are going to need God when you lose everything. Don't you ever try to put your life ahead of God because you are going to need God when life deals you a heavy blow trying to save your life for your own way of living. Finally, don't you try to put your health ahead of God because you are going to need God when the doctors tell you there is no more they can do or they give you a bad report. The prodigal son needed God. I need God, and you need God.

Can I be real with you today? You need God. Whether it's sunshine or rain, whether it's victory or defeat, whether it's high or low, whether you are sick or well, whether you are rich or poor, whether you win or lose, whether you are lost or saved, whether you are married or single, and whether you are gay or straight, you need God. The prodigal son had the blessings of God, but let's be real: the blessings will turn against you when you don't worship God, from whom all blessings flow. All of us need God. Thank you, Holy Spirit. Let's examine Psalm 127:1 NSB.

A - Unless the Lord builds the house (I need God).
B - They labor in vain who built it (I need God).
C - Unless the Lord guards the city (I need God).
D - The watchman stays awake in vain (I need God).

With God, nothing stands.

The prodigal's made-up mind didn't happen in his father's house nor in the faraway country. He made up his mind in the hogpen. When you traffic in sin, it will lead you to a place where you lose what is important to you, just to reveal to you how much you need God. I've discovered that some people have to lose it all before they seek the Lord.

All of us have gotten this advice from our parents and grandparents: "Don't let life catch up with you before you turn to God and learn how to trust Him as your Lord and Savior" (2 Corinthians 6:2). He made up his mind when he was in a mess. He made up his mind when all hell broke loose. He made up his mind when there was no relief in sight. He made up his mind when he found himself in stinging mud. He made up his mind after everybody helped him lose everything he had, and they left him down to nothing. He made up his mind after he realized that it didn't take very long for him to waste all that his father gave him. He made up his mind after the devil enticed him, used him, and tried to destroy him in a place where sin was out of control. This is what happens when sin catches up with you. It's a fast track to homelessness that almost drives you to insanity. It doesn't matter what drove him away from home; he just needed to go back home.

He couldn't fix his life by staying in the hogpen. When you're sitting there in a mess, a made-up mind says, "I wish I can go back to how things used to be with God and my father." The father helps us by never leaving his post, even though the son did. The prodigal son ministers to us by saying when you distance yourself from God, no matter what the situation is, you did the leaving.

The prodigal son made up his mind to leave his father's house, and now the situation has changed. Life caught up with him, and it's that type of life that's squeezing him to make up his mind again, but this time, it's to go back home.

For several moments, let's talk about the power of a made-up mind. To encourage you, to inspire you, and to also motivate you, let's drill home the thought that all you need to make it in this life is you and God.

One of the powerful things on this earth is a made-up mind, and I've discovered that until you reach that crossroad where you can tell nobody but you, "My mind is made up," but you are still vulnerable to the traps around you. A made-up mind has the essential ingredients to move anyone to victory and success. Every passion, every dream, and every goal begin with a made-up mind, and if you desire it long enough, nothing on earth can stand in your way.

I remember that as a young teenager in high school, I saw someone riding their horse to school, and I wanted to do the same thing, but I didn't have a horse. I made up my mind that I wanted a horse, so I asked my mother who had limited resources to buy me a horse. She looked at me with a strange look on her face, but it wasn't an impossible look.

I kept asking until she said, "I don't know where to buy a horse."

I said, "I know where to buy one. I know someone who's selling one. All they want is $250.00 for that horse." To my surprise, she handed me the money, and I was able to buy that horse to ride to school, while my brothers and sisters rode the school bus. I had to stick to a made-up mind to get that horse. I never asked my mother where she got the money from or if she borrowed the money, and until this day, I still don't know. She has gone on to be with the Lord. A made-up mind resulted in buying a horse to ride to school.

As a child, you also displayed a made-up mind and never took no for an answer, and you carried on terribly until you got what you wanted. Maybe one day, you will get the opportunity to share your made-up mind experience.

I want to share with you six nuggets of a made-up mind.

1. *Building an alertness to barriers*

Your whole mind, body, and spirit join forces to block any signs of holding you back. You cross over hurdles, and you go through locked doors. You sense when something or someone is trying to block your way, and you do something immediately to stop it because your mind is made up.

2. *Silencing the negative voices*

You are very careful with whom you get information from, and you don't accept anyone who does not see or feel or is encouraged by what the Lord is showing you. You close your ears to anyone who criticizes, objects to, or opposes your plans to do something positive. You have a made-up mind to achieve your goals.

3. *You endure life's pain*

You have made up your mind to go through whatever it is to be all you can be in Christ Jesus. Pain is part of the process. God knows firsthand what pain is. Psalm 56:8 NLT says, "You keep track of all my sorrows." This is quintessentially the very thing we want from God, for him to see us and deal and eradicate our pain while we are striving to get ahead in life with a made-up mind.

4. *You confront the fears in your life*

Fear is an uneasy feeling. It's an alarm that signals when we feel threatened. I'm referring to that paralyzing fear that undoubtedly is a spirit of fear. Paul wrote in 2 Timothy 1:7 saying, "God has not given us a spirit of fear, but of power and love and of a sound mind." When fear is in front of you, face it head on. Begin to break down the nature of your fear. Are you afraid of failures that will lead to criticism, rejection, or inadequacies? First, get your eyes off your fears, and put them on Jesus, and ask the Lord to give you the help you need, and try to be specific with God: "Lord, help me right now in this situation." When you need a fear buster, memorize the Word of God that strengthens you. A made-up mind becomes fearless.

5. *Celebrate the difference in you*

In 2 Corinthians 5:17, Paul says, "Therefore, If anyone is in Christ, he is a New Creature; old things have passed away; behold, all things have become new." You have to know who you are. You become an encouragement to the new you. You are not and like everybody else, and you are not a carbon copy of somebody else. You are the original with a made-up mind.

6. *You are what you think*

It is the feeling or belief that one can have faith in or rely on someone or something. *Self-confidence* means "feelings or beliefs that you have on yourself." So if you connect them both, it is the thoughts and beliefs that you have on yourself for the betterment of your own future. Proverbs 23:7 says, "For as he thinks in his heart, so is he." Our minds are powerful, and our thoughts shape who we are and we will become. Do not copy the behavior and customs of this world, but let God transform you into a new person by changing the way you think. Then you will learn to know God's will for you, which is good and pleasing and perfect. As you think, you change the physical nature of your brain. As you consciously direct your thinking, you block out toxic ways of thinking and replace them with spiritual and healthy thoughts. I've discovered that changing the way you think changes your perspective, which also changes how you act in the world. A made-up mind chooses to see reality, and they have the power to change their reality by shifting their focus. Let's say it this way: what you allow into your mind determines your reality and eventually your legacy. I am a firm believer that whatever we think and feel at any given time is basically our request to the world for more of the same. It is so important that we make sure that we that we are sending out signals that resonate only with what you want to be, do, and experience. Again, your mind is a very powerful thing, and most of us take it for granted. We believe we are in control of what we think because our thoughts seem to fly in and out all day long. You are what you think, and that's the secret power that we have when we have a made-up mind.

CHAPTER 6

The Returning-to-God Type of Son

And he arose and came to his father.

Let's begin to place ourselves in this story in Luke 15:11–32. You as the prodigal son have gone through so many different phases in life. It's a possibility that you could be in one of those right now. You chose to leave your Father's house so you could do everything on your own. You are fed up with everybody telling you what to do, and spiritually, you are in a turmoil, a battle, a tug-of-war with God the Father. Everything that has been given to you or what you inherited has been wasted on bad choices you made away from your Father's house. You're down to nothing, nowhere to go and no one to turn to. You are the reason that you are at the lowest place in life, which is unbearable, especially when the pigs start talking to you. What will the pigs say about you? That you degraded yourself to be like an animal and now you're in the same situation like some people you saw and talked about, at your worst condition?

Somebody reading this book knows what it's like to turn your back on God and then watch everything you have go downhill so fast it blew your mind. The prodigal son struggled physically on the outside, the worldly part of himself, but what about the inside, the inner person, the soul part of him? When the cravings for God wake up on the inside of us, you will discover that all the worldly things that pulled you out there were no good at all. You will discover that life that God gives you is not to be wasted in a world that will be soon destroyed. Life is so fragile, and the wrong choices will leave you empty on the inside. Many of you know that nothing in this world can satisfy the hunger for God but God himself. The Bible tells us in Romans 12:1–2:

> I beseech you therefore, brethren, by the mercies of God, that you present your bodies a living sacrifice, holy, acceptable to God, which is your reasonable service. And do not be conformed to this world, but be transformed by the renewing of your mind, that you may prove what is that good and acceptable and perfect will of God.

Somewhere in all our lives, something showed up that had more pulling power than God, and in our own way, we left the teachings of God's Word, to do those things that go against the will of God. Atheist and modern enlightened people have no need for God. Selfish people have no need for God. Modern-day cults have no need for God. They all say, "We can manage well without God. Who needs him?" What a way to distance ourselves from God and lose intimacy with and fellowship with him. It's through our sins, our transgressions, our iniquities, our shortcomings, and our ungodliness that we stop serving, stop worshiping, stop praying, and stop reading God's Word, and that's our way of denying him.

God does not force us to obey him or even serve him or go against our will. Every one of us has a choice to stay with God or leave God. He lets us have our own will. You can rest assured that somewhere along the way, during your worst moments, we begin to realize how far we are away from God. We begin to realize that all the worldly things that we deemed important are just stumbling blocks in the way of what is really important, our life with Christ. When your heart is fixed and your mind is made up, something in the heart says, "I want to go back to God, to my Father's house. There's rest in my Father's house, and in God, there is peace that surpasses all understanding."

How many of us have experienced relatively good lives and seem to have it all together but still yearn for this deep unrest when our souls wake up and thirst for something that is more than what the world offers? Finally, we come to the point where you say, "I will arise and go to my Father" (Luke 15:18).

God shows us just where the prodigal son ends up, sitting with the pigs, and they too know that something is wrong. He's far away from the Father. I've discovered that where the prodigal son is right now is not his worst condition. I believe his most critical condition was his loneliness, his emptiness, and his realization that he was really lost, without his Father, without God. Lost people without God will go into darkness, so dark, they can't see their way out.

So in the prodigal's mind right now is "Go back to the Father." Jesus Christ took all our sins to the cross, hung, bled, died, and rose early that third day for us to go back to our Father. The glory of God's house is waiting on us. Every time I see a cross, I think of Calvary because it was there that God changed the whole course for mankind and he stood ready to meet us at our crossroads of life.

It doesn't matter where you are in your lostness or how terrible your condition is, torn or dirty, lost and broken, or torn up from the floor up. He gave his only begotten Son as a sacrifice for you, where you will not remain lost in your sin and transgression. Luke 19:10 says, "He came to seek and to save that which was lost." God will bring you home, but you must have a made-up mind to go. God put so much on the line just to save man, and man cannot take it for granted. It's a blessing to go home.

The prodigal son wanted to go back to his father. He turned away from his father, but to our surprise, the father didn't turn away from his son. Like God, the father waits, the father watches, and the father hopes that the day will come when his son will come back home.

A good friend of mine who pastors a church in Augusta, Georgia, Pastor Richard Smith, used to say, "Whenever I go back to North Carolina, my parents would always keep the light on, on the front porch, because they knew I will always come home." The light on the front porch is a reminder of parents' continuous love for their sons and daughters. The prodigal son saw the light on the porch, and he knew then that the father's love was still there and he was never forgotten nor forsaken. That reminds me, even when we are lost and far away from God, *God* is still our Father, and Jesus is on the main line; you can call and tell him what you want.

When the son was in a condition that he could not handle, he remembered his father and saw the glory of God shining on the porch. When the shadow of death hangs over you, that is the perfect time that God will call us to repent and come back to him, our holy Father. Luke 15:7 says, "There will be more joy in heaven over one sinner who repents than over ninety-nine just persons who need no repentance." Every lost son or daughter who makes up their mind to come back to the Lord has the assurance of Jesus: "The one who comes to me I will by no means cast out" (John 6:37).

Deep down in his heart, the prodigal son knows that by his wrong choices in life, he has thrown away more than an inheritance; he has thrown away a blessed relationship with his Father. Jesus says, "But when he was still far off, his Father saw him." The father continuously watched for his son to come back home, and that's why he was able to see him afar and had compassion on him, ran, and embraced and kissed him.

In our modern way of living, as well as the Middle Eastern culture, this was no way for a father to behave. You know how some people do it; they would have made that son cry for mercy, waddle in the dust, and yelled and screamed at him, before they will forgive him.

Thank God that this was not in this father's heart; instead, he ran out and embraced him and threw his arms around him, validating what was already on the son's heart: "My father loves me no matter what."

This was no time for fault-finding or augmentative gestures. The son just acknowledges his wrongdoing when he says, "Father, I have sinned against heaven snd before you. I am no longer worthy to be called your son. Treat me as one of your hired servants."

There is no longer any doubt in his mind about his father's love, a love so merciful and full of compassion. We are looking at a father who displays the appearances of the Divine Mercy:

1.   The father reveals his faithfulness to God, his commitment as a child of God, and his godly stance as a father who cares, supports, disciplines, and provides for his family.
2.   The father's compassion for his son's downfall to sin.

God reveals to us in this story that what we see happening to the prodigal son is a grace that accompanies and works alongside repentance to restore the son's true dignity as a forgiven son. From start to finish, there is one word that strengthens the love of God, and that is what I called *agape*.

I've discovered that agape love is able to reach way, way down to every son or daughter, to every human calamity, and to every form of ungodliness connected to sin. The result is that the person who is the object of mercy refuses to be humiliated but overjoyed to be found again, realizing that life has value beyond measure. After all that the father has been through, the joy that he displays now has never lost purpose. He still sees good that was always there from the beginning.

Jesus's real intention for the father of the prodigal son is to be a revelation of the heart of God the Father. The parable of the prodigal son challenges us to behave like the merciful father and reach out to those who are estranged from us, in fact, to go the extra mile.

God's compassion is revealed in his Son, Jesus, not to show me how willing God is to care for me or to forgive me for my sins and offer me life and happiness. Jesus invites me to become like God and to have and show the same compassion to others as he has shown us.

Every child of God is challenged to be men and women who encourage homecoming, no matter how distant we or other people are from home. I am always struck when I read and reread this parable because it impresses me always to have great hope. It's like a dialogue between our weakness and the patience of God; it is a dialogue that if you have it, it will grant you hope.

God's patience has a way of calling in us the courage to come back home, no matter how many mistakes and sins one may have in their life. It is there in the wounds of Jesus that you and I are truly secure and we encounter the enormous amount of love in his heart.

The two aspects of a good father are the following: (1) a father forgives with all his being; (2) a father is always ready to restore a son his dignity after repentance, to come back into fellowship with him.

CHAPTER 7

A Son Worthy of Celebration

I want to begin this chapter looking at the special times that we celebrate. We celebrate Christmas and New Year. We celebrate birthdays and anniversaries. We celebrate Mother's Day and Father's Day. We celebrate 4th of July, Memorial Day, Labor Day, etc. We celebrate these days not because someone has fallen in their life from living on the wrong side of life. We celebrate these days not because someone's family has been torn apart and brought back together again. We celebrate these days because of customs and traditions and just for the joy of getting together and enjoying family no matter what one has been through.

We celebrate Thanksgiving by drinking and partying and eating ourselves sick or bent over from a hangover. We celebrate Black Friday so we can shop until we drop to get the best deals on the market. We celebrate our sports teams no matter what their ranking is or their outcome or situation. Many of us celebrate our favorite movie stars, rich and famous, who damage their careers by drugs, sexual molestation, domestic violence, murder, etc. We have created a whole economy around celebrating how they can create bigger and better events or technology or entertainment or social organizations that now condition us to expect bigger celebrations to overwhelm us.

Let's be real: How much time have we spent or guilty are we of unworthy celebrations? What about attending a funeral of someone who has done evil all of their life and they died a horrific death. Do we go to the funeral to celebrate that a child of God has gone home to be with the Lord? What about celebrating that coworker on the job who was always at odds with others, always causing confusion, and always involved in disputes? What about that student at school who fights against the teachers, fight other students for no reason, disrupts the class, curses the principal out, or even hits a teacher and bring drugs to school and that parent who throws a party to celebrate their birthday? What about that church member who disrespects the pastor and deacons, refuses to obey the bylaws, gets out of control in every business meeting, cannot work with other members, and sets bad examples for the young adults yet we celebrate them because they were one of the first members to join the church? What about that abusive husband who disrespects his wife by cheating on her with another woman and that woman ends up pregnant with his child? That woman then goes to the wife's job to confront her in the midst of her employees. The wife gets fed up with her husband's actions that've been constantly ripping their marriage apart. She calls her husband to tell him that we are done. He then shows up on her job and shoots her a number of times, and then in a shootout with the police, he's killed. They then have a funeral to celebrate his well-lived life.

I'm going to let you decide if all the examples given warrant being called unworthy celebration. However, let's consider some worthy celebrations. Luke 15:10 says, "Jesus said, 'I tell you, there is rejoicing in the presence of the angels of God over one sinner who repents.'" You have to understand that one of the most important roles of angels is praising and glorifying God. There is joy over one who is rescued out of the hands of Satan and his angels.

With the help of the Holy Spirit, let's list some worthy celebrations:

1. When the people of God begin to share the Word of God with one another and they become more mature in their walk with God
2. When Christians bring their unsaved friends to church and they get saved and baptized to identify with Jesus's death, burial, and resurrection

3. When Christian parents by faith begin to spiritually nurture their children through enrichment programs to have a closer relationship with God
4. When you become a Christian example to someone who has been through some horrific experiences in their life and they are now enriching someone else's life
5. When prodigals leave home to search for life at its best and they wind up broke, busted, and disgusted yet they return home asking for forgiveness and truly repentant in their heart
6. When our Christian youth finish high school, go off to college, graduate, and return home, to pursue careers as doctors, lawyers, dentists, teachers, motivational speakers, or business owners or even in professional sports or retire in the military, and still, they honor God and their families.

On his return, the father treats his son with a generosity far more than what he deserves and what he expected. This celebration means giving his son a makeover. He is given the best robe, a ring on his finger, and sandals to put on his feet. I've discovered that clothing in the Bible was symbolic of a person's change in status. Clothing and accessories represent the prodigal son's rebirth; he was dead and is alive again and in his newfound state was lost and is found. The record from Jewish philosophers tells us that "parents often do not lose thought of their children who live wasteful lives." And based on our knowledge of God, he also takes thought of those who live a misspent life. God gives us time for reformation while keeping within the bounds of his merciful nature.

The joy that the father displays describes divine love, the boundless mercy of God, and God's refusal to limit the measure of his grace.

Let's not miss the teaching in the story that gives us the basis for God's celebration.

God loves mankind so much that he sent his Son to earth to die for our sins (John 3:16). Furthermore, he is "longsuffering toward us, not willing that any should perish but that all should come to repentance."

God's love and repentance is the cause for celebration and accep-tance. From this parable, we can draw a number of spiritual lessons:

1. We can be a genuine son of the Father, who is spiritually alive, and be lost through sin. We can turn our backs on our heavenly Father and leave him on our own free will. Mortal sin is a real possibility.
2. Mortal sin inevitably sends us into a far worse state than we were in before.
3. We can return, go back to the Father, and be accepted by him with joy. God is always ready and eager to welcome us back to him with forgiveness, no matter what we have done.
4. No child of God who has never fallen should never resent those who come back to God. Instead, we should share in their joy.
5. You are secure in God, and your heavenly reward is not threatened. God loves you the same as he loves those who come back to him through dramatic conditions.

God has a way of seeing men and women that you and I cannot understand. It's like we are made of glass. God sees all our past, pres-ent, and future. The compassion of God is followed by swift move-ments. He is slow to anger, but he is quick to bless. It doesn't take God long to consider how he shall show his love to those who repent. It was all taken care of a long time ago in the eternal covenant. God does not need to prepare for man's return; that was done on Calvary. God comes in swiftly in the greatness of his compassion to help everyone in their need to come back to him through repentance.

Let's make sure that we understand why the father celebrated the return of his son. First is because Jesus is showing that God alone deserves the glory. Surprisingly, the son could not take the credit for this lavish celebration. Everybody there was commenting on the great love the father had for his son, who was undeserving of it all. The party blessed the son, but it showed the uniqueness of the father. Jesus also made a point to the pharisees that "I find those that are lost, I welcome those who know that I am full of grace and mercy and they know they need me." Our works can never take the place of the amount of sin we committed, which caused us to turn away from God.

Second, Jesus is teaching us how to expand our joy in God. The pharisees would not hear Jesus, so they carried on in their own way of thinking. The older son lost his joy because he was full of selfishness. He felt like he deserved more than what he was getting. I've discovered that when some people think they deserve something from God, they end up despising God the most. They have a way of seeing God like Santa; they get angry at God when they don't get what they ask for, and they rate that on how many times they have been on the good list. When you as a child of God begin to realize that every good and perfect gift is given by the God of grace, then we are filled with thankfulness and joy to God because he gives us what no one deserves. How many times have you embraced the grace of God, despite knowing that you didn't deserve it? That's when we stop lying to ourselves that we deserve anything good from God. When you are God-centered, you quickly realize that salvation is meant to exalt our Savior; it elevates our joy for God because we live our lives centered on our Lord and Savior. Never think that God will throw you a party because of your works; you will end up a joyless misinformed Christian.

Last, Jesus introduces us to the Gospel. In our salvation, God exalts himself for his glory. Just knowing God and what he has done for us humbles ourselves enough to allow him to have all the honor by depending on nothing else but his grace; it increases our joy.

Celebrating the prodigal son's return is a wonderful picture of the Gospel of Jesus Christ. Thank you, Lord, the God who is love is nothing like the people of the world. People will exalt themselves by putting others down. God exalts himself by lifting other people up (Philippians 2:6–11). Jesus, in the form of God, came down from heaven and literally died for all of us low-down sinners. He came down to man, not only to save man but exalt himself by saving man.

In the words of the late Jonathan Edwards, "God in seeking His glory seeks the good of His creatures." God is so awesome and so full of everlasting love and kindness that he can place himself at the middle of everything good or bad that he is exalted foremost through him by producing our good. Through it all, God is seeking to please himself (his highest goal) by being overwhelmingly lavish and compassionate and loving to his people.

Dietrich Bonhoeffer wrote, "Since fallen man cannot rediscover and assimilate the form of God, The only way is for God to take the form of man and come to him."

I've discovered that happiness in the Word of God is always a by-product of seeking to honor God more than seeking our own happiness. Notice that the Word of God never says: "Blessed is he who thirst and hunger for blessedness." It always says the man who is blessed is the one who seeks something greater than their own happiness, in other words, something more God-honoring.

If the prodigal had worshiped God more in his life than personal happiness, he would have accomplished both. Yet he chose to seek personal happiness and not worship God and didn't accomplish anything. I have discovered that the happiest people in this world are those who have given up trying to be worldly happy but have worked hard to live for something greater.

When we focus on the wrong things in life and not the good God desires for us, we actually lose focus of glorifying God, and it causes us to lose everything in the process. When you rearrange the process and start elevating your personal satisfaction over your glorification of God, you wind up a loser. The Bible says the truth is what sets you free. The prodigal never believed in what God was doing, and he also rejected the reasons why God was doing what he does, and it robbed him of the truth about life. If the prodigal looked for truth, he would have found comfort at the end. Yet he looked for comfort first and found neither one (comfort nor truth). And wishful thinking leads to despair.

If we separate God's reasoning from his blessings, we lose the real blessings in the process. There is a cure for our deepest contentment, and that is to seek ultimate contentment by magnifying God. When our good becomes the main ideal rather than God's glory, we hinder our good in the process.

God throws us a lifeline when we waddle in the sea of selfishness. Yes, that lifeline is the grace and mercy of God to live a life pleasing to him. When we live for the purpose of God's glory, God throws out the lifeline to reel us in from the life-destroying elements of the world, to set us free to live above the choices that end up drowning us.

The prodigal thought that life was thrown to him just for him to live his life the way he wanted to, and he cut the cords that were to pull him into safety. Like the prodigal, if we hope to stay connected to our lifeline, we will discover that the solution to all discontentment is to realize that even the lifeline, benefits, and blessings come from God, and he deserves the glory for it all. Would you agree that our proper response to the good that we do is not to become prideful but rather give humble adoration to the one who made it all happen in the first place? And that's God. When you and I take that to heart, we would not only be more humble, but we would have more spiritual power as well.

That's where the prodigal missed it. God gives spiritual power to those who give him all the glory. The father is giving God all the glory. Please don't miss the point. This doesn't mean that the way to power is to glorify God. That kind of thinking elevates power over glorifying God. But when we are true to God, our motives are true, and our giving God the glory is true. Now, our spiritual power stands up in our weak and discouraging moments.

God is using the father to give him the glory by celebrating the return of his son. The father is also celebrating how God uses him in forgiving his son. The father forgives just like God, and it frees him up to do a higher degree of love. The father was willing to free his son of the debt he owed to him, to release him from the punishment he really deserves. He had a higher reason to choose love, and in his heart, God was that reason. The Father chose not to hold on to the hurt done to him; he gave it to God for his own sake, and it pleased God. He chose to be free from the weight of unforgiveness. When the father desired not to throw his son into a prison of regret, he also kept himself from his own personal prison of torture. The prodigal son returned home shattered from the way he treated his father, owned up to his faults, and asked to be a hired servant over being a son—a son worthy of celebration.

CHAPTER 8

A God of Mercy

Let's define mercy. The Bible reveals to us that *mercy* means "his pity, compassion, and kindness toward mankind." His mercy shows up in our lives when we are saved, and then God constantly shows mercy in forgiveness.

Here is a graphic definition of mercy by Jonathan Edward:

> God is pleased to show mercy to His enemies, according to His own sovereign pleasure. Though He is infinitely above all, and stands in no need of creatures; yet He is graciously pleased to take a merciful notice of poor worms in the dust.

Millard Erickson wrote in *Christian Theology*:

> God's mercy is His tenderhearted, loving compassion for his people. It is His tenderness of heart toward the needy. If grace contemplates humans as sinful, guilty and condemned, mercy sees them as miserable and needy.

The following are translations of *mercy* in Hebrew:

1. *Racham* means "to love or have compassion, to have a disposition of mercy" (Psalm 116:5).
2. *Kapporeth* means "ransom," and it's associated with the "mercy seat" in the Bible (Exodus 25:22).

3. *Chesed* means "goodness," "kindness," or "mercifulness" (Psalm 18:25).

Inquiring minds want to know the definition in Greek:

1. *Eleemon* means "to have pity on," "to show compassion," or "to be merciful" (Matthew 5:7).
2. *Oiktirmos* means "the idea of divine forbearance in showing compassion and passing over sins" (Romans 12:1).

Author and blogger Tim Challies describe *mercy* as follows:

> God acting patient. It is God extending patience to those who deserve to be punished. Mercy is not something God owes to us, by definition mercy cannot be owed, but is something God extends in kindness and grace to those who do not deserve it.

In mercy, God is holding back the judgment of correction for a later time. God chooses not to bring justice immediately. It's the mercy of God that's shocking because the wrong we have done and the punishment we deserve are held back from us. Mercy is beyond our understanding. It was at the cross where God's wrath and mercy met so man can be transformed and made to fit eternity.

Someone says, "What is the Mercy Seat?" At first, it takes us back to Exodus, while the second comes at the end of the Gospel according to John. Exodus 25:22 describes the description of the tabernacle and specifically the key piece of furniture, the ark of the covenant. At the very top is the mercy seat, and stationed on either side are two cherubim (Exodus 25:19). It was at this very place, at the mercy seat, where God meets with his people. Exodus 25:22 says, "There I will meet with you."

If we connect Romans 3, it reveals the Greek word used for the Hebrew word for "mercy seat." The Greek translation of the Old Testament uses the word *hilasterion* to translate the Hebrew word.

The Greek word *hilasterion* normally is translated as "propitiation" in the New Testament. Propitiation only appears a number of times in the New Testament such as in Romans 3:25, concerning Christ and his work of redemption. Paul declares that God gave forth Christ "as a propitiation." Christ is the only righteous acceptable sacrifice that pleased God for the salvation of mankind.

Stay with me! In John 20:12, Mary Magdalene comes to the burial site of Christ only to find it empty. She then saw two angels in white, sitting where the body of Jesus was laid, one at the head and one at the feet. As we look back at Exodus 25, there stood two angels who took their place at either end of the mercy seat. Now, let's tie up the loose ends. God's desires to meet with his people and the blood of the spotless lamb were the only means by which the meeting was made possible. The mercy seat of the Old Testament, and the blood sprinkled on it by the high priest—thank you, Jesus—prefigured Christ to come. Christ did come, and he made the sacrifice, hung, bled, died, and rose from the dead. Therefore, the tabernacle was real. The ark of the covenant was real. The mercy seat was real. The cross was real. The empty tomb was real. The resurrection was real. Therefore, Christ is our mercy seat. It's through Christ where God meets us. God is known as a God of mercy and grace.

The Bible reveals to us that God is merciful even to the worst offenders, sinners, and lawbreakers. It means that even though God knows about our guilt, he doesn't always give the whipping we deserve. Let's elaborate in Romans 3:23–24, which says, "All have sinned and fall short of the glory of God, and are justified freely by His grace through the redemption that came through Christ Jesus." Let me say it this way: We are all sinners and do not meet the standards of righteousness that God intends us to have, but thank God, through his mercy and grace, he provided a way for our sins to be forgiven through our belief and accepting Christ as our Savior. We did nothing to deserve it. Tied in with grace, mercy is shown because God loves us and only asks that we accept his son by faith.

The God of mercy calls for our attention in Micah 6:8: "He has shown you, O man, what is good. And what does the Lord require of you? To act justly, and to love mercy and to walk humbly with your God"—life-changing words to all of us in these days and times. God's mercy is endless. It was available in the prodigal's time as well as in our time. God's mercy is shown upon those who need it. Man was born with a sinful nature, and rather than condemn us, God is merciful in that he willingly withholds the punishment we so rightfully deserve.

In the Bible, God shows many illustrations of his mercy. God showed mercy to Lot and his daughters, allowing them to leave Sodom before it was destroyed (Genesis 19:14–16). God's mercy of compassion was put on display by rescuing the children of Israel from bondage in Egypt and taking them into the Promised Land (Exodus 15:13).

The steadfast love of God is coupled with his mercy: "But God, being rich in mercy, because of the great love with which He loved us, even when we were dead in our trespasses, made us alive together with Christ, by grace you are saved" (Ephesians 2:4–5).

God requires us to be merciful and forgiving to others, no matter what they have done. He did it for us. Thank God for his Word because it's in the Word of God that we get a glimpse into the heart of God. It is there that we can set eyes on his mercy without minimizing the power of his might and see the life-changing method he uses to save us. By nature, we assume that God shows mercy by accident or weakness. But in all actuality, when God shows his mercy, he does intentionally so we could not only see how sovereign he is but also see into his goodness. Not overlooking his greatness, we see his gentleness. Not diminishing his power, we see also his tenderness.

I've discovered that God's mercy not only shows us who he is, but it also shows us something about ourselves. We see that we have been shown mercy, not deserving of his favor, but we deserve his judgment. Your cry for mercy indicates your admission that you are guilty of ill-deserving but for the mercy of God.

Throughout the Bible, we are not the first to peek into God's heart and catch a glimpse of his Fatherly position back then. God made the world to travel over and over on the rich revelations of his mercy. The first glimpse of God's mercy came through Moses, who asked God to show him his glory. God said to him, "I will make all my goodness pass before you and will proclaim before you my name 'The Lord.' And I will be gracious to whom I will be gracious, and will show mercy on whom I will show mercy" (Exodus 33:19).

When Moses asked God to show him his glory, God manifested his goodness in grace and mercy and put it on display for all Israel to see. We know that Israel's righteousness did not supersede Pharaoh nor the Egyptians, but God's mercy on Israel was not given based on their goodness or works. God was telling Moses that Israel's bad actions did not have a factor as to whether to show mercy on them. God is free to show mercy on whoever he wants to, whenever he wants to, and how long he wants to, and God has chosen to be merciful to his chosen generation.

As you stroll down the chapter in Exodus 34:6–7, God passes Moses by and says:

> The Lord, the Lord, a God merciful and gracious, slow to anger, and abounding in steadfast love and faithfulness, keeping steadfast love for thousands, forgiving iniquity and transgression and sin, but who will by no means clear the guilty, visiting the iniquity of the fathers on the children and the children's children, to the third and the fourth generation.

I have discovered that God is not unjust, nowhere in his mind is the thought of clearing the guilty nor to sweep sin under the rug. And the excitement of it all and for his glory is mercy. God would be unloving to his people if he didn't get angry when others assault and do harm to them. Yet even in that, he's slow to anger. God's righteous response to evil is his wrath, but it's nowhere in his heart. Justice is the light pole that holds up mercy.

Another glimpse of the merciful God is seen in the times of David. King David, Israel's great psalmist, found himself in a position where he had to cast himself on the mercy of God. Psalm 51 records David's confession: "Have mercy on me, O God, according to your steadfast love; according to your abundant mercy blot out my transgressions" (Psalm 51:1). The Bible tells us that when David realized that he had sin against God, by numbering the people, the prophet Gad offered three options to be disciplined by God, saying, "Shall three years of famine come to you in your land? Or will you flee three months before your enemies, while they pursue you? Or shall there be three days of plague in your land?" It's here that David again experience the glimpse of God's heart because he knew where to go during his distress: "Let us fall into the hand of the Lord, for His mercies are great, but do not let me fall into the hands of man" (2 Samuel 24:14).

Let's travel back down the dark paths of history found in the book of Lamentations. The people drifted away from God because their hearts were hard. After the Babylonians besieged, conquered, and decimated Jerusalem, the city was crushed and famished. These were the darkest times of the prophet Jeremiah. Chapter 3 records what was in his heart and how the pain was exposed and how he didn't see any hope. Even in our darkest moments, faith can still shine, and this is where Jeremiah gets a glimpse into the heart of God concerning mercy. He says:

> Remember my affliction and roaming, the wormwood and the gall. My soul still remembers and sinks within me. This I recall to my mind, therefore I have hope. Through the Lord's mercies we are not consumed, because His compassions fail not. They are new every morning; great is your faithfulness, "The Lord is my portion," says my soul, "therefore I will hope in Him."
> (Lamentations 3:19–24)

Here is the prophet Jeremiah in the dark moments where the people of God tempt to abandon hope, and he's pointing to the mercies of God that never cease and that they are new every day.

Finally, let's consider the apostle Paul and how he got a glimpse into the heart of God concerning mercy. It was in Jesus's time that Paul was called into the ministry because of God's mercy (1 Corinthians

7:25). Jesus is the mercy of God made human (the mercy of God to us). Jesus made a request in the gospels, saying, "Have mercy on me," which is exactly what God did in his perfect life, his sacrificial death, and his miraculous resurrection. God extends mercy, not just to Israel but to all mankind. Moses saw, David fell on, and Jeremiah wept for it. Paul actually saw through the death, burial, and resurrection of Christ, and he marveled. Paul stated in Romans 9:16, "But of God who shows mercy." In other words, God's mercy shows us his heart, and that's what Paul shows us in Romans 9:22–23, which gives us a deep glimpse into the heart of God. Underneath the covers, we find mercy.

Paul puts it in the form of a question; not that he's unsure or unbelieving, but it's the effect that it takes because it is so awesome and overwhelming to think about. Here it is:

> What if God, desiring to show His wrath and to make known His power, has endured with much patience vessels of Wrath prepared for destruction, in order to make known the riches of His glory for vessels of mercy, which He has prepared beforehand for glory.

God is not only sovereign and uncompromising in his justice, but he is the mercy-dealing God, who welcomes us not only to take a glimpse at his awesome authority and his almightiness but to set our focus on his mercy and observe it in his heart.

Psalm 111:4 says, "He is full of compassion." Isn't it amazing that how often, when we relate to God, some of us are not really sure who he is? We think we know, so let me help you out: God is not part mercy; God is not sometimes mercy; God is not every now and then mercy; God is mercy in the highest form.

Psalm 115:5 says, "Gracious is the Lord and righteous." Yes, our God is merciful. It refers to who he is. Psalm 119:64 says, "The earth, O Lord, is full of your mercy." Psalm 119:156 says, "Great are your tender mercies, O Lord." Ephesians 2:4 says, "He is rich in mercy because of His great love."

I have talked to many people who believe that they have blown it so bad in their life, they have no hope, and they lost hope. Maybe you heard some people say, "If God only knew what I am really like and what I have done in my life, there is no way I could be what God is asking me to be." God is never asking you to be anything less than who he is. He gives us all we need, and he's not asking you to work for it apart from faith. A merciful father restored a lost and fallen son, and mercy was so plenteous and forgiven that it warranted a celebration unbelievable.

CHAPTER 9

Undiscovered Reality

Up to this point, the celebration blessed the prodigal son. He was restored back to fellowship with his father. I wish we could say, "Wow, what a wonderful ending." We love it when the people who hurt us repent and ask for forgiveness. They were able to show us their heavy heart from the guilt of doing wrong. They couldn't hide it any longer. There were no more pretending that everything was all right. Everything was real.

Please don't forget that Jesus told this parable for the benefit of the pharisees and the scribes, a story about them. Unfortunately, the older son had their characteristics and selfish ways. His attitude mirrored theirs to a tee. The pharisees displayed a kind of self-righteous, self-promoting, and self-willed attitude, totally different from the goodness and grace of God. Very importantly, they believed that they had God's favor because they thought they earned it, point-blank.

The Bible shows that Jesus forgave tax collectors, liars, drunkards, thieves, prostitutes, and the unfortunate. The pharisees didn't agree with that nor learned from that nor was compassionate toward them, but they were furiously upset and angry—a similar picture of the older son.

Actually, the older son covered up his resentment, and the father never saw it. When the father threw a celebration, everyone was there but the older son. He was outside, waddling in anger. Some of us are just like the older son. You too didn't like it when your own siblings made a mess of their life, yet they are welcomed back home and treated like nothing ever happened and celebrated. You, on the other hand, never left home and did all the right things to stay on

49

the good side of your parents. You obeyed your parents faithfully and never gave them any trouble, yet the one who didn't care about anything is celebrated.

My question is: "Was the Father blinded by his own desire to do what's right and was never able to notice the motives of the older son?" What would your critics say about you if you did what this father has done? All of us have some critics waiting to criticize everything we do. Would you agree that people who live by the rules should receive their reward? This world has its fair share of people who have walked away from their homes and their community, just to live according to their own undisciplined ways. Should they be able to come back and somehow reap the rewards of other people's hard work?

The lesson that I learned from this father is, when you celebrate the one son who seriously disappointed you, you should also have celebrated the older son for his faithfulness. Doing it one way sends a signal that foolishness and stupidity and wastefulness and selfishness pay off and faithfulness and obedience get overlooked. We reside in a world where moral standards have fallen through hard times and where people are constantly living to do their own thing regardless. We reside in a world where social decay is running rampant, our youth are dropping out of school, family structure is fallen apart, family abuse is overwhelming, some fathers are out there doing their own thing, and kids are raising themselves.

The father of the prodigal son stood against loose self-indulgence and more rule-following, more self-discipline, and more personal accountability and respect for those in authority over them. I personally understand fatherhood because I am a father, who raised two sons and three stepkids. I'm pleased to know this father. He encouraged me to continue to apply his fatherly wisdom in this day and time.

There is a battle going on between the no class and the upper middle class. The upper middle class represents the older son, who underestimates and uses other people's faults against them to make himself shine brighter. There are overwhelming cases of the older brother's class campaigning against the lower class to live the way they live righteously. The actions of the father exposes the truth that people of the older brother's mindset are just as stained as anybody else. No matter how one lives or what one does, nobody is perfect and so righteous above anybody else.

I'm a firm believer that the older son wasn't working to please his father but for his own self-aggrandizement. The rod between good and evil does not travel between people and classes. It finds its way through the human heart. I believe the father made up his mind to restore his son on his own without the help of anybody else. This way, meeting his son would be real and untouched by other people's opinion. This wasn't the job of the older son to do. He would not have handled it the way the father would have. Just the wrong look from the older brother would have caused the younger son to go back to what he wanted deliverance from.

When you discover what is really in a person's heart, sometimes, it will blow your mind if it is overwhelmingly cruel. In all actuality, both sons were in the hogpen. The younger son was in the hogpen in a far country, and the older son was in the hogpen in his father's house.

God bless this father because he teaches us to never overlook the motives in those around us, even those in our own household. Is there recovery for these two sons? Yes, there is. Thank God for those he uses to create projects to bring siblings together for more important goals in rebuilding fractured relationships. At the end of the story, the father gives each son a valuable gift, a gift so precious that it resembles the grace and mercy of God. The prodigal son gets a second chance to dedicate himself faithfulness, obedience, and self-discipline. The older son gets to refocus the wrong use of self-ambition and works to please God and his father. Both of them can now embrace a more meaningful relationship as brothers—a relationship that they could never achieve by themselves.

When the older son tells his father, "All these years, I've been working for you and never disobeyed your orders," the pharisees were probably thinking, "Okay, here is someone we can relate to. He's like us."

Jesus placed within this story a description of the older son to drive home the point that the younger brother wasn't the only one who showed disregard to the father. Both were critical in their own way. Can you imagine having these two sons in your home, one who is totally lost but didn't think he was and the other who was lost but stood behind his goodness?

Shame on us when we look at reprobate sinners and we can see how badly they need Jesus but fail to see the pride in our own hearts after sitting in the church week after week. So many church folks resemble the older brother syndrome, which tends to see themselves as good and the others as bad.

Just for the sake of clarity, let's look at a few characteristics of the older son and see if we can make sure that we ourselves do not tempt to fall into the same trap of resentment, anger, and indignation:

1. He thought because he did everything right, he deserved a blessing. Have you ever asked God to heal you because you deserved it? Are you one of those who think you will make it to heaven because you attend church every Sunday? Maybe you are the one who keeps a checklist of all the good you do so you can tell God about it. Have you ever felt shortchanged by someone, especially God?

2. His motive was to get all he could get for himself, not to display love for his father. Our relationship with God should be about pleasing him, serving him, loving him, and growing closer to him, even though we don't get everything we deserve. We must love God more than loving to get something out of him.

3. He couldn't forgive nor forget his brother's sin. When your standards become higher than God, you too will never forgive anyone who does wrong in their life. You too would say to your father, "That's your son, but not my brother." Why is it that we judge and hold on to pass sins against one another? Didn't God forgive you for the wrong you done? If the answer is yes, then forgive others.

4.   His anger of resentment stopped him from sharing in the joy of the father. Our hearts must be broken by the things that break the heart of God. It's all about seeing this thing through the eyes of God because you can't trust your own eyes if you haven't been spiritually changed. I pray that we search our hearts and examine ourselves inwardly rather than outwardly.

Psalm 19:12–14 ought to be our constant prayer:

> But who can discern their own errors?
> Forgive my hidden faults.
> Keep your servant also from willful sins;
> May they not rule over me.
> Then I will be blameless,
> Innocent of great transgression.
> May these words of my mouth and this medita-
>   tion of my heart
> Be pleasing in your sight,
> Lord, my Rock and my Redeemer.

It's never too late for anyone to jump off the circulatory wheel of life and begin living the abundant life, that is, a close fellowship with the Father every day of our lives. Say what you want, but it doesn't get any better than this. Every purpose that God wants to fulfill in your life will come from a direct relationship with him.

Let's stick a pin in three eye-openers for our lives:

1.   You can call yourself a Christian and still harbor wrong intentions and wrong thoughts concerning other people.
2.   You can call yourself a Christian and still lose focus that cripples your relationship with God.
3.   You can be a Christian and still have a slave mindset.

Our motivation is to worship God because we love him. We neither worship nor serve God for rewards but seek him who wants to reward us. Yes, the older son, and many modern-day older sons, is somewhat like Jonah—self-centered, rude in what comes out of their mouth, and more concerned about fairness and justice for themselves than having compassion and mercy for others.

God refuses to let us get away from separating ourselves from evangelism and telling others about Christ or helping the poor and hurtful in order to point them to Christ. The prodigal son's older brother teaches us to always be at a point where you can see enough of yourself and with what you find, turn it around for the glory of God.

I feel a need to pray: Father, I can see something in me that resembles the older brother, and I don't like it. Fill my heart anew with your joy, and blot out any notion of how deserving I am compared to other people. Father, give us compassion for younger brothers who have fallen and have a desire to come home. Father, help us to be able to help them rather than defend our churches who are disturbed by their unchurch ways. Father, forgive me for my whining and complaining about others when I have issues myself, and make us more responsible sons, who can share in our Father's joy and heart of mercy. In Jesus's name, amen.

Let me share some truth here: mercy extends forth her hand to misery, and grace saves men who are sinners, demerited, unworthy, and worthless; it deals with those who think of themselves as righteous, and not the object of compassion, but who see the unrighteous, the undeserving, and the guilty as the only people for the infinite mercy of God. Grace has nothing to do with rules and fairness. Grace has everything to do with unmerited favor and love that "covers a multitude of sins" (1 Peter 4:8). God's grace does not make sense from a fleshly point of view. It seems unfair and more outrageous. When they think of underserved charity, it makes them angry.

There are times when embracing mercy has to be a conscious effort on our part. Unfair as it may seem, there will be moments where we have to choose to let go of our anger and what has been done, to move ahead in life.

The prodigal son's brother was just as human as the prodigal son himself. He wasn't being a bad guy because he got upset. He didn't understand why his father had to go for an all-out celebration instead of a quiet time at home. This story is about stepping back to see the other person's side and not being so quick to go with our anger. Experience has taught so many of us that we don't always know the whole story or walk in the other person's shoes, and sometimes, you have to take a timeout and think about that, regardless of how right we are in our feelings.

I am reminded of James 3:14–16:

> But if you have bitter envy and self-seeking in your heart, do not boast and lie against the truth. This wisdom does not descend from above, but is earthly, sensual, demonic. For where envy and self-seeking exist, confusion and every evil thing are there.

You see, bitterness is connected to envy and selfishness, and it can cause a whole lot of other things to grow. I am further reminded of Hebrews 12:14–17:

> Pursue peace with all people, and holiness, without which no one will see the Lord: looking carefully lest anyone fall short of the grace of God; lest any root of bitterness springing up cause trouble, and by this many become defiled; lest there be any fornicator or profane person like Esau, who for one morsel of bread sold his birthright For you know that afterward, when he wanted to inherit the blessing, he was rejected, for he found no place for repentance, though he sought it diligently with tears.

Here we are told that bitterness can make it impossible to repent, even if you think you want to do things right.

This story leaves the older brother without a conclusion. Will he change? This is what Jesus was trying to get the pharisees to do—

change and to feel the conviction for themselves. So what should the pharisees do, and what should the older son do? I'm literally talking to every one of us, every one of us who has become pharisees along with the older brother syndrome because of our sin. When our hearts become hard and bitter due to our mean, selfish, and resentful ways, we also need to repent. When you cannot rejoice over the salvation of other people, other people who have done us wrong, wronged other people, and did wrong in the eyes of God, and if we do not want to see them saved, then we need to repent and rejoice over the salvation of anyone who was lost and now found. The Bible says, "While we were yet sinners, Christ died for us." Jesus rose from the dead so that you and I could be resurrected and we, too, could be restored and made whole again.

Let's pull the curtain close while considering this thought: never overlook your part in a situation gone bad. Why? Because, sometimes, we think we know better and are better than anyone else. We, too, have squandered the grace of God and traded it in for worthless worldly treasures. Our eyes quickly stretch wide open when we realize that we are unworthy, living beneath our God-given potential, only to live a pig lifestyle, which reveals that we are sinful, rebellious, down to nothing, destitute, and swallowing in stinking mud, yet down deep inside us, there is an uncut cord that compels us to run back into the arms of our God of grace and mercy, and he saves us.

For by grace you are saved, and let every sinner and lost person and selfish, inconsiderate people say, "Amen."

Let me throw in some murrayology: I felt sorry for the prodigal son when he got to the point that he thought it best to leave the love of his father, take his inheritance, and waste it by any means possible. Now that many of us have recovered from our faraway experiences, whether it was in a far country or right there in our homes, we know God never left us nor had forsaken us. And then what about those other siblings who chose to stay in place and continued to labor no matter what? How would you feel if a person like that returns home and is treated as if nothing ever happened? Now you fall into the older brother's shoes who actually covers up his own story only to exploit his goodness above grace. Come off your high horse; you're not all that and a mountain dew. Secrets are killing Americans' homes. What's the real story of your home? Some of us were as twisted as both sons, yet we had a loving Father who didn't give up on us.

My forty-five-minute experience led me back home to a loving mother and eventually to giving my life to Christ. I'm a living witness that you can raise a family with both sons living in the home. As a father, I could not show favoritism to either one. I pray that as they raise their sons, they took some nuggets from a father who never lost love for them and who made them feel they were always welcome back home, good or bad. In some homes across this nation, true family love has fallen on hard times.

It's the end of this story but never the end of your story. May God bless the readers of this book.